KING
QU

This I-SPY book belongs to:_____

This book tries to highlight, very briefly and simply, the main dates, happenings and achievements of all the monarchs of Britain over 1,200 years, from the Anglo-Saxon King Alfred the Great, who ruled Wessex from 871–899, to our present day Queen Elizabeth II, who has reigned for 60 years. Among the 57 monarchs in this book, only six have been queens. Since the Norman Conquest in 1066, there have only been eight names used by the kings: William, Henry, Stephen, Richard, John, Edward, James and Charles.

Our next two kings will probably be Charles and William. There have only been 10 different families on the throne in over 1,000 years, and incredibly, they are all related. Our present queen can trace her ancestry right back to those feuding nobles of the Middle Ages. Some of her children even bear the same titles: the first Duke of York was created in 1385. Looking back in history, some of our kings appear bloodthirsty and violent but judge each ruler in the times in which they lived. Kings killed brothers and cousins to keep the throne strong, Henry VIII abandoned one wife after another in order to produce a son and stabilise the monarchy. And

some of our rulers were truly great by any standard: Alfred the Great brought stability to a country under attack from the Danes, and during the reign of Elizabeth I, England saw a great flowering of trade, culture and literature. Victoria presided over the growth of the British Empire and the economic change brought about by the Industrial Revolution. Today our monarchy is respected throughout the world; governments come and go but the monarchy continues as a symbol of this country's great history and heritage.a great flowering of trade, culture and literature. Victoria presided over the growth of the British Empire and the economic change brought about by the Industrial Revolution. Today our monarchy is respected throughout the world; governments come and go but the monarchy continues as a symbol of this country's great history and heritage.

How to use your I-SPY book

As you work through this book, you will notice that it is arranged chronologically (in date order) of the Kings and Queens of the United Kingdom. You need 1000 points to send off for your I-Spy certificate (see page 64)

but that is not too difficult because there are masses of points. Count your I Spy points for any building, statue, wall tablet or plaque with a connection to the monarch that you see. You can score points for multiple

I-Spys. As you make each I-Spy, write your score in the box and double if you can answer the question correctly. Check your answer against the correct one on page 63.

ELIZABETH II

Born 21 April 1926

Reign 6 February 1952–

HRH Queen Elizabeth II celebrates her Diamond Jubilee in 2012. She is married to Prince Philip, the Duke of Edinburgh, and they have three sons and one daughter, eight grandchildren and two great-grandchildren. Her main home is at Windsor Castle, and she spends time at Buckingham Palace in London, Sandringham House in Norfolk and Balmoral Castle in Deeside, Scotland. She is a constitutional monarch, meaning she acts as head of state but is answerable to Parliament.

I-SPY points: 25

Date: _____

Windsor Castle is the Queen's main home; it was severely damaged by fire in 1992.

THE FUTURE OF THE BRITISH MONARCHY

The eldest son of HRH Queen Elizabeth II and Prince Philip is Charles, Prince of Wales and he will inherit the throne. He married Lady Diana Spencer in 1981; she died in a car accident in Paris in 1997. They had two children, William and Harry.

Both William and Catherine studied at St Andrews University in Fife, Scotland

I-SPY points: 20

Date: _____

When Prince Charles ascends the throne, William will become Prince of Wales and will one day be king himself. He married the commoner Catherine Middleton in 2011 at Westminster Abbey. They now hold the title of Duke and Duchess of Cambridge.

The Queen's only daughter is Anne, the Princess Royal, who has two children with her first husband

Prince Charles married Camilla Parker-Bowles in 2005 at Windsor Guildhall.

I-SPY points: 20

Date: _____

Captain Mark Phillips. Peter Phillips is married to Canadian Autumn Kelly. Zara Phillips is a champion horsewoman who recently married rugby star Mike Tindall. Princess Anne is now married to Vice-Admiral Sir Tim Laurence.

Prince Andrew, the Duke of York, married and divorced Sarah Ferguson. They have two daughters, Beatrice and Eugenie.

The Queen's youngest son, Prince Edward, Earl of Wessex, has been married to Sophie Rhys-Jones since 1999; they have two young children, Louise and James.

I-SPY points: 15

Date: _____

There are Royal Apartments at Kensington Palace and Clarence House in London.

SAXON KINGS

Alfred the Great 871–899

Edward the Elder 899–924

Aethelstan 925–939

Edmund I 939–946

Eadred 946–955

Eadwig 955–959

Edgar 959–975

Edward the Martyr 975–978

Ethelred II 978–1016

Edmund Ironside 1016

PLANTAGENET KINGS

Henry II 1154–1189

Richard I 1189–1199

John 1199–1216

Henry III 1216–1272

Edward I 1272–1307

Edward II 1307–1327

Edward III 1327–1377

Richard II 1377–1399

LANCASTER KINGS

Henry IV 1399–1413

Henry V 1413–1422

Henry VI 1422–1461 and 1470–1471

INTERREGNUM

James I 1603–1625

Charles I 1625–1649

Oliver Cromwell (*) 1649–1658

Richard Cromwell (*) 1658–1659

STUART KINGS AND QUEENS

Charles II 1660–1685

James II 1685–1689

William III 1689–1702 and

Mary II 1689–1694

Anne 1702–1714

(*) Lord Protector

English Kings and Queens at a Glance

DANISH KINGS

Canute 1017–1035

Harold I (Harefoot) 1035–1040

Harthacanute 1040–1042

SAXON KINGS

Edward the Confessor 1042–1066

Harold II January–October 1066

NORMAN KINGS

William I 1066–1087

William II 1087–1100

Henry I 1100–1135

Stephen 1135–1154

YORK KINGS

Edward IV 1461–1470 and 1471–1483

Edward V April–June 1483

Richard III 1483–1485

TUDOR KINGS AND QUEENS

Henry VII 1485–1509

Henry VIII 1509–1547

Edward VI 1547–1553

Mary I 1553–1558

Elizabeth I 1558–1603

HANOVER KINGS AND QUEENS

George I 1714–1727

George II 1727–1760

George III 1760–1820

George IV 1820–1830

William IV 1830–1837

Victoria 1837–1901

WINDSOR KINGS AND QUEENS

Edward VII 1901–1910

George V 1910–1936

Edward VIII abdicated 1936

George VI 1936–1952

Elizabeth II 1952–

ALFRED THE GREAT

Born c.848

Reign 23 April 871–26 October 899

Parents Ethelwulf, King of Wessex and Kent, and Osburh

Children Four or five including Athelfleda and Edward the Elder

Famous for burning his cakes, Alfred was born at Wantage in 848 and became one of England's greatest kings. He fought the Danish invaders of eastern England and finally defeated them at Edington in Wiltshire in 878. He brought prosperity to his kingdom of Wessex and during his reign, he founded 25 towns, including Shaftesbury, Wallingford and Barnstaple, built schools and monasteries, introduced new laws and expanded the navy.

I-SPY points: 35

Date: _____

A monument stands to Alfred on The Broadway in Winchester, erected in 1899.

EDWARD THE ELDER

Born c.871/872

Reign 26 October 899–17 July 924

Children Possibly 14

King Alfred's eldest son continued his father's good works, despite putting down a rebellion before he could claim his throne. In 906 he made peace with northern warlords at Tiddingford in Bedfordshire and he raided the north-east, beating the Vikings at Tettenhall. Edward united the kingdoms of Wessex and Mercia (Midlands), and extended his kingdom northwards. He had time to marry three times and have 14 children!

Where is Tettenhall?

Edward was buried at Hyde Abbey; only the gatehouse now stands.

I-SPY points: 20, double with answer

Date: _____

SAXON KINGS BEFORE ALFRED THE GREAT

Five Saxon kings had ruled England before Alfred: they were his grandfather, father and three brothers. Their names were Egbert (802-839), his son Ethelwulf (839-858) and three older sons of Ethelwulf: Ethelbald (858-860), Ethelbert (860-866) and Ethelred (866-871), who was later made a saint. They ruled over Wessex and battled constantly with invading Vikings as well as warlords from Northumbria and Mercia. The kingdom of Kent was won for Wessex in 825 and dynastic marriages were made in Europe, setting the scene for Alfred's long and successful reign.

AETHELSTAN THE GLORIOUS

Born c.894/895

Reign 2 August 925–27 October 939

Children None

Aethelstan won land in York and Northumbria. He signed the Treaty of Penrith with Scots King Constantine II in 927, before defeating him in 934 at Caithness and Brunanburgh to become the first king of all Britain.

Which English county is Malmesbury in?

I-SPY points: 20, double with answer

Date: _____

Aethelstan is buried at Malmesbury Abbey.

EDMUND I, THE MAGNIFICENT

Born c.922

Reign 27 October 939–26 May 946

Parents Edward 'the Elder' and Edgiva

Children Three including Eadred and Eadwig

Brave Edmund inherited a united Britain but had to battle to maintain his kingdom. The Vikings at York, the Welsh and the Scots rebelled against his rule but he defeated them all. In 945 he entrusted land around Strathclyde to Malcolm, King of Scotland.

I-SPY points: 35

Date: _____

Edmund died in a fight at Pucklechurch in Gloucestershire and was buried in Glastonbury Abbey.

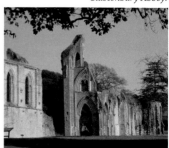

EADRED

Born c.923

Reign 26 May 946–23 November 955

Parents Edward 'the Elder' and Edgiva

Children None

Following Edmund's murder, Eadred ruled Wessex, the Danelaw around York, Mercia and – after he had Viking rebel Erik Bloodaxe thrown out in 954 – Northumberland. Although still turbulent, England was relatively peaceful.

I-SPY points: 35

Date: _____

It is believed that the Mortuary Chest in Winchester Cathedral may contain Eadred's remains.

EADWIG

Born c.941

Reign 22 November 955–1 October 959

Parents Edmund I 'the Magnificent' and Elgiva

Children Three including Edward and Ethelred

Young, foolish Eadwig did not rule his turbulent kingdom well. His reign was marked by infighting with his family and the clergy; in 957 lands north of the Thames were given to his brother Edgar to rule.

I-SPY points: 35

Date: _____

Eadwig gave money towards the building of Bath Abbey.

EDGAR THE PEACEFUL

Born c.943

Reign 1 October 959–8 July 975

Parents Edmund I 'the Magnificent' and Elgiva

Children Three including Edward and Ethelred

On the death of his brother Eadwig, Edgar ruled a united Britain. A powerful king, he maintained peace by alliances with rebel leaders, built boats to protect against Viking sea attack and divided England into shires.

I-SPY points: 35

Date: _____

A statue to Edgar the Peaceful stands on the front of Lichfield Cathedral.

EDWARD THE MARTYR

Born c.962

Reign 8 July 975–18 March 978

Parents Edgar and Athelfleda

Children None

The downfall of the Saxon kings began with Edward. He was deeply religious and upset the wealthy clergy by taking away their powers. Civil war nearly broke out between warring nobles and Edward was murdered. In 1008 he was made a saint.

I-SPY points: 35

Date: _____

Edward was assassinated at Dorset's hilltop Corfe Castle in 978.

ETHELRED II, THE UNREADY

Born c.968

Reign 18 March 978–23 April 1016

Parents Edgar and Elfrida

Children 16 including Edmund Ironside and Edward the Confessor

After the Battle of Maldon in 991, Ethelred paid danegeld (bribes) to the Vikings to stop them invading the north of England. Danish Sweyn Forkbeard was declared king in 1013 but died weeks later in February 1014. Ethelred fled to France after his downfall but made a brief return.

Where did the Vikings come from?
I-SPY points: 20, double with answer

Date: _____

Danish invaders fought the English army, led by Byrthnoth, the Ealdorman of Essex at the Battle of Maldon, leading to defeat for Ethelred.

EDMUND IRONSIDE

Born c.988

Reign 23 April 1016–30 November 1016

Parents Ethelred II and Elgiva

Children Two including Edward the Atheling

Edmund fought the Danes in London and defeated them at Brentford before forging a treaty with Canute, son of Sweyn Forkbeard, after the Battle of Assandun. Mercia and Northumberland went to the Danes while Edmund kept Wessex, East Anglia and London. He died suddenly soon after.

I-SPY points: 35

Date: _____

Edmund was crowned King of England at St Paul's Cathedral in London.

SWEYN FORKBEARD

Sweyn Forkbeard was a Viking king who ruled Denmark from 959-986. His repeated invasions of England in the 1000s led to the weakening of the monarchy and his adoption as king in late 1013. He died in strange circumstances after just a few weeks in power in February 1014; his son Canute continued to fight the British.

CANUTE

Born c.994/995

Reign 1017–1035

Parents Sweyn (Forkbeard) and Gunhilda

Children Five including Harold I (Harefoot) and Harthacanute

On the death of Edmund Ironside, Danish Canute became king of England. He was a strong ruler and under his leadership British trade, the church and the arts flourished. His empire stretched across northern Europe. King Canute is wrongly associated trying to stem the tide, when in fact he was demonstrating that no man, not even a king was able to do this.

I-SPY points: 20

Date: _____

Canute died in Shaftesbury and there is a memorial plaque to him in the abbey.

NEAR THIS SPOT A.D. 1028
Canute
REPROVED HIS COURTIERS

HAROLD HAREFOOT

Born c.1016

Reign 12 November 1035–17 March 1040

Parents Canute and Elgiva

Children One

On the death of his father Canute, Harold claimed the throne but two years of feuding with his half-brother Harthacanute passed before he was crowned in 1037. Apart from a few raids on Scotland and Wales, he managed little in his reign.

Why was Harold called "Harefoot"?

I-SPY points: 35

Date: _____

Harold Harefoot was buried in the churchyard of St Clement Danes in the City of London.

HARTHACANUTE

Born c.1018

Reign 17 March 1040–8 June 1042

Parents Canute and Emma

Children None

Canute's legitimate son was King of Denmark when Harold died. He took the English throne peacefully but increased taxation to pay for his fleet; Worcester was burnt to the ground in retaliation for tax riots. He is believed to have been murdered.

I-SPY points: 35

Date: _____

Harthacanute was mentioned in the 12th-century Ramsey Chronicle as generous and principled.

EDWARD THE CONFESSOR

Born c.1003

Reign 8 June 1042–5 January 1066

Parents Ethlered the Unready and Emma of Normandy

Children None

The seventh son of Ethelred the Unready was brought up in Normandy, France and restored Wessex kings to rule following Harthacanute's death. He was seen as a weak king, but most of his reign was peaceful, with no further invasions by the Danes. Rivalry between Wessex lords and Norman aristocrats led to bickering and exiles from Edward's court and Northumberland warlords attacked Wales.

I-SPY points: 30

Date: _____

Edward built the first abbey at Westminster in London.

HAROLD II

Born c.1022

Reign 5 January–14 October 1066

Parents Godwin, Earl of Wessex and Gytha of Denmark

Children Seven

The son of Godwin, Earl of Wessex, succeeded Edward on 6th January 1066 and died in battle with William the Conqueror in October the same year. Those few months saw victory against the Norwegians at Stamford Bridge near York. William met the English troops near Hastings and Harold was killed; the first English king to die in battle and the last of the Anglo-Saxon kings.

How did Harold die in the Battle of Hastings?

I-SPY points: 30, double with answer

Date: _____

Norman kings from France came to power in 1066 after the Battle of Hastings as depicted by the Bayeux Tapestry.

WILLIAM I, THE CONQUEROR

Born c.1027

Reign 26 December 1066–9 September 1087

Parents Robert I, Duke of Normandy and Herleva

Children Ten including Robert II, Duke of Normandy, William II, Stephen, Count of Blois and Henry I

The Witan – Anglo-Saxon Parliament – offered William the throne after his victory against Harold II at the Battle of Hastings. He spent six years harshly suppressing rebellions in East Anglia and Exeter and then introduced the feudal system of land ownership. William started the Domesday survey to extract taxes from his subjects, introduced a legal system, reorganised the church and provided England with a stable government.

What was the feudal system?

I-SPY points: 30, double with answer

Date: _____

William founded York Castle in 1068; it was the site of heavy fighting with the Danes and Scots.

WILLIAM II

Born c.1056

Reign 9 September 1087–2 August 1100

Parents William I 'the Conqueror' and Matilda of Flanders

Children None

Nicknamed "Rufus" due to his bright-red hair, William II spent much of his reign battling his eldest brother Robert, Duke of Normandy, for the English throne. He defeated Robert in 1088, secured the frontiers with Wales by building Cardiff Castle and a chain of forts along the border and crushed Scottish rebels. William maintained peace by stripping his nobles of power and died out hunting in the New Forest.

I-SPY points: 30

Date: _____

William died in the New Forest when out hunting. His memorial is near Canterton.

HENRY I

Born 1068

Reign 3 August 1100–1 December 1135

Parents William I the Conqueror, and Matilda of Flanders

Children Four legitimate, only Matilda survived (at least 25 illegitimate)

The youngest and cleverest son of William the Conqueror married into the house of Wessex to gain English support and defeated his brother Robert, Duke of Normandy in 1106. Henry issued a Charter of Liberties for his people, and reorganised the courts and the tax system. He nominated his daughter, Matilda, as his successor after his son William drowned at sea.

I-SPY points: 30

Date: _____

Robert, Duke of Normandy, was held captive at Cardiff Castle after his rebellion in 1106.

Stephen came from Bois. Which country is that in?

I-SPY points: 30, double with answer

Date: _____

STEPHEN

Born c.1096/1097

Reign 22 December 1135–April 1154

Parents Stephen, Count of Bois and Adela

Children Five plus five illegitimate

On Henry's death, the throne bypassed Matilda for his nephew, Stephen of Blois. After 70 years of stable Norman rule, unrest marked his reign: the Scots and Welsh invaded, Matilda invaded from France and civil war followed. Lawless rebels destroyed crops, creating famine, and warring nobles fought their neighbours. To stop the violence, Stephen signed a treaty agreeing on Matilda's son Henry as his successor.

Stephen's army defeated Matilda at the Rout of Winchester in 1141.

EMPRESS MATILDA

Matilda was promised the throne of England as the daughter of Henry I. She married the Holy Roman Emperor, Henry V, and later the Count of Anjou. When she was overlooked on her father's death, a period of civil war began in England called The Anarchy. She possibly ruled England briefly in 1141 but Stephen was soon back in power.

HENRY II

Born 25 March 1133

Reign October 1154–6 July 1189

Parents Geoffrey V the Fair, Count of Anjou and Matilda the Empress

Children Eight including Henry 'the young king', Richard I and John plus at least 12 illegitimate

The first Plantagenet king was son of Empress Matilda, a French aristocrat whose empire stretched from Scotland to Spain. He took power away from the nobles and reclaimed the north from Scotland. He created a permanent military force and the jury system still used today. However, Henry lost control over the church after quarrelling with the Archbishop of Canterbury Thomas à Becket, who was murdered in 1170.

I-SPY points: 30

Date: _____

Thomas à Becket was assassinated on the altar steps inside Canterbury Cathedral in 1170.

RICHARD I, THE LIONHEART

Born September 1157

Reign 6 July 1189–6 April 1199

Parents Henry II and Eleanor of Aquitaine

Children None, possibly two illegitimate

A great soldier, Henry's second son spent just 10 months of his 10-year reign in England, which he used as a source of income for his crusades in the Holy Land. He took part in the third crusade but on his return journey was captured by the Duke of Austria, who sold him to Holy Roman Emperor Henry VI. He was imprisoned until a ransom was paid in 1194, which cost England 65,000 pounds of silver and gold.

I-SPY points: 20

Date: _____

 During Richard I's absence, whilst at the crusades, England was ruled by Richard's brother, John.

An equestrian statue of Richard the Lionheart leading a crusade is outside the Houses of Parliament in London.

JOHN

Born 24 December 1167

Reign 6 April 1199–19 October 1216

Parents Henry II and Eleanor of Aquitain

Children Five, including Henry III, plus 12 illegitimate

Wicked King John lost much of the Norman empire to the king of France, fell out with the church and was excommunicated, and raised harsh taxes to fund his battles in France. A revolt led by Archbishop of Canterbury Stephen Langton in 1215 forced John to sign the Magna Carta, agreeing to uphold the power of the church, the aristocracy and the laws of the land. He soon broke his word.

What does Magna Carta mean?

I-SPY points: 30, double with answer

Date: _____

The Magna Carta was signed in 1215 at Runnymede in Surrey by the king and his statesmen.

HENRY III

Born 1 October 1207

Reign 18 October 1216–16 November 1272

Parents John and Isabella of Angoulême

Children Nine including Edward I

Henry ascended the throne aged nine; at first capable deputies ran the country and expelled invasions from France. Later he raised taxes to fund his overseas campaigns and ignored pleas for reform. His brother-in-law Simon de Montfort led a rebellion in 1258 and introduced a 'parliament' to force him to take advice from his barons. De Montfort was murdered in 1265 but his parliament formed the basis of today's House of Commons.

I-SPY points: 30

Date: _____

Henry III was a patron of architecture, building Salisbury Cathedral during his reign.

LOUIS VIII

Louis VIII was King of France from 1223–1226 and invaded England at the request of English barons to de-throne King John. In July 1216 he lay siege to Dover and Windsor. But John died and his infant son Henry III inherited the throne; Louis VIII was forced to return to France, where he resumed his crusades.

EDWARD I

Born 17/18 June 1239

Reign 16 November 1272–7 July 1307

Parents Henry III and Eleanor of Provence

Children Nineteen including Edward II

Edward was Henry III's son and both a statesman and soldier. He created the 'Model Parliament' of 1295, bringing together the nobility, clergy, knights and city leaders in the Lords and Commons. Judicial reforms saw the introduction of Conservators of the Peace and different courts for different crimes. Edward conquered Wales and made his son first Prince of Wales, but was unsuccessful in Scotland, waging war against William Wallace and Robert the Bruce.

I-SPY points: 30

Date: _____

Richard I built Caernarfon Castle as part of a defensive line of castles to keep the Welsh out of England.

I-SPY points: 30

Date: _____

Edward II was murdered at Berkeley Castle in Gloucestershire in 1327

EDWARD II

Born 25 April 1284

Reign 7 July 1307–20 January 1327

Parents Edward I and Eleanor of Castile

Children Four

Despite founding colleges at Oxford and Cambridge, Edward was tyrannical and feeble. He had unsuitable favourites, and silenced most opponents by murdering them. He exiled his greatest enemy, Henry of Lancaster. Robert the Bruce defeated him at the Battle of Bannockburn in 1314, and Scotland remained independent until 1707. When his queen, Isabella of France, deposed him in favour of their son with the backing of exiled noble Roger Mortimer, Edward was imprisoned.

EDWARD III

Born 25 April 1312

Reign 7 July 1327–20 January 1377

Parents Edward II and Isabella of France

Children Thirteen plus at least three illegitimate

The long reign of Edward III saw the beginning of the Hundred Years War with France. It started in 1338 with him claiming the French throne, but was primarily about opening trade routes in Europe. The outbreak of bubonic plague in 1348 saw half of England's population killed in two years. It was also a time of social reform: English replaced French as the official language and Parliament met regularly.

I-SPY points: 30

Date: _____

The Black Death was introduced to England through the port of Weymouth in 1348.

 ## THE HUNDRED YEARS WAR

The struggle between France and England lasted from 1338 until 1453. In the early years the British had victories at Sluys (1340), Crecy (1346) and Poitiers (1356) with Edward III's son, called the Black Prince for his bravery. English fortunes waned during the reign of Richard II, but rose with Henrys IV and V. Henry V won at Agincourt (1415) and signed the Treaty of Troyes in 1420, but with Joan of Arc on side, France gained the upper hand. By 1453, all that the English owned in France was Calais.

RICHARD II

Born 6 January 1367

Reign 22 June 1377–29 September 1399

Parents Edward 'the Black Prince' and Joan, Countess of Kent

Children None

Young Richard inherited social unrest and increasing prices and wages, which caused the Peasants' Revolt in 1381, led by Wat Tyler. He did temporarily stop the war with France in 1396, but was deposed by once-exiled Henry of Lancaster when he tried to overturn Parliament. His death at Pontefract Castle in 1400 marked the beginning of the Wars of the Roses over succession to the throne.

I-SPY points: 30

Date: _____

Richard II died at Pontefract Castle, either by starvation or an axe to the head.

THE WARS OF THE ROSES

The so-called Cousins' War lasted through the reigns of seven English kings. The trouble started with Edward III, who had 13 children, with four sons, several daughters and many cousins surviving him. He was succeeded by his grandson Richard II, who was the son of the Black Prince, but Richard was deposed by Henry of Lancaster in 1399. The Lancaster house was then deposed in turn by their York cousins in 1461. Yorkist Richard III was killed at the Battle of Bosworth in 1485, and distant cousin Henry VII came to power, marrying Elizabeth of York and unifying the houses of York and Lancaster under the Tudor banner.

He was the head of a strong dynasty that lasted for 146 years and saw the long reigns of two of our greatest monarchs, Henry VIII and Elizabeth I.

The battles were at St Albans (York, 1455), Blore Heath (York, 1459), Ludford Bridge (Lancaster, 1459), Northampton (York, 1460), Wakefield (Lancaster, 1460), Mortimer's Cross (York, 1461), St Albans (Lancaster, 1461), Ferrybridge (York, 1461), Towton (York, 1461), Hedgeley Moor (York, 1464), Hexham (York, 1464), Edgecote Moor (Lancaster, 1469), Losecote Field (York, 1470), Barnet (York, 1471), Tewkesbury (York, 1471), Bosworth Field (Tudor, 1485) and Stoke Field (Tudor, 1487).

Middleham Castle was home to the powerful Neville family, Earls of Warwick and Salisbury, during the Wars of the Roses.

HENRY IV

Born c.30 May 1367

Reign 30 September 1399–20 March 1413

Parents John of Gaunt and Blanche of Lancaster

Children Six including Henry V

Henry of Lancaster faced rebellions all through his reign. The half brothers of deposed Richard II rose immediately against him, and they were severely punished. The noble families of Percy and Mortimer rebelled and many aristocrats and clergymen were executed for treason. Welsh leader Owen Glendower led an uprising that rumbled on until 1410, and the Scots waged continual war in the north. Henry eventually quietened his kingdom and there were no more civil wars until 1455.

What colour was the Lancaster rose?

I-SPY points: 20, double with answer

Date: _____

The Archbishop of York rebelled against Henry at York Minster.

31

HENRY V

Born 16 September 1387

Reign 21 March 1413–31 August 1422

Parents King Henry IV and Mary de Bohun

Children One, Henry VI

A keen soldier, Henry V immediately renewed the Hundred Year's War with France. He won a great victory at Agincourt in 1415, which crippled France, led by the insane Charles VI. Following the Treaty of Troyes in 1420, Henry married Charles's daughter Catherine and his son was declared heir to both the English and French throne. He died suddenly in 1422, possibly from dysentery, while still campaigning in France.

I-SPY points: 30

<u>Date:</u> _____

Henry V was born at Monmouth Castle in 1387.

HENRY VI

Born 6 December 1421

Reign 31 August 1422–4 March 1461 and 30 October 1470–11 April 1471

Parents King Henry V and Catherine of Valois

Children One

English king at nine months old and French ruler two months later, Henry's family reigned for him for 20 years. Weak government saw a decline in English interests in France and acute fighting in the Wars of the Roses. Intrigue was all around; Henry lost the Battle of Towton in 1461 to the Duke of York, who became Edward IV, only to be deposed himself by the Earl of Warwick, who briefly reinstated Henry.

Why was the Earl of Warwick called the "Kingmaker"?

I-SPY points: 25, double with answer

Date: _____

Henry VI founded Eton College in 1440 and Kings' College, Cambridge the following year.

EDWARD IV

Born 6 December 1442

Reign 4 March 1461–3 October 1470 and 1471–1483

Parents King Henry V and Catherine of Valois

Children Six including Edward V and Richard, Duke of York (the Princes in the Tower)

During his first reign, Edward IV struggled for power against a formidable enemy, the Earl of Warwick. He fled to Burgundy but returned in 1471 to reclaim the English throne at the Battle of Tewkesbury, where Henry VI was later killed. His second reign was relatively quiet; in 1475 he invaded France and was paid a bribe by King Louis XI to return home.

I-SPY points: 30

Date: _____

Edward IV triumphed against the House of Lancaster at the Battle of Tewkesbury.

EDWARD V

Born 2 November 1470

Reign 9 April–26 June 1483

Parents Edward IV and Elizabeth Woodville

Children None

Edward was 12 when he ascended the throne and only survived for two months. His evil uncle, Richard, the Duke of Gloucester was named as his protector but sent him and his younger brother to the Tower of London. Richard probably had the boys murdered before seizing the throne for himself. Years later in 1674, two skeletons of young boys were found in the Tower; these may be the bodies of the young princes.

What colour was the Tudor rose in the Wars of the Roses?

I-SPY points: 50

Date: _____

The two young princes Edward and Richard were imprisoned in the Tower of London.

RICHARD III

Born 2 October 1452

Reign 26 June 1483–22 August 1485

Parents Richard Duke of York and Cecily Neville

Children One plus at least four illegitimate

Richard claimed the throne under suspicious circumstances following the imprisonment of his young nephews in the Tower of London. Although an able soldier and clever administrator, he was ruthless and deeply unpopular. He put down a rebellion by the Duke of Buckingham and was then killed at the decisive Battle of Bosworth Field in 1485, which put the Tudor Duke of Richmond in power and virtually ended the Wars of the Roses.

I-SPY points: 30

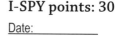

Date: _____

King Richard III apparently took his last drink from the well at Bosworth Field.

HENRY VII

Born 28 January 1457

Reign 22 August 1485–21 April 1509

Parents Edmund Tudor and Margaret Beaufort

Children Eight

The Tudor dynasty began in bloodshed but heralded a more peaceful era. Henry restored order to the nation, introduced heavy taxes and fines and removed power from his squabbling nobles. He married Elizabeth of York, wed his eldest son Arthur (who died young) to Spanish princess Catherine of Aragon and his daughter Margaret to King James IV of Scotland, forming important political allies. Trade and exploration increased and national stability was restored.

Which other English prince, who later became king, was married to Catherine of Aragon?

I-SPY points: 30, double with answer

Date: _____

Henry VII spent his early years at Pembroke Castle in Wales.

HENRY VIII

Born 28 June 1491

Reign 21 April 1509–28 January 1547

Parents King Henry VII and Elizabeth of York

Children Three Mary, Elizabeth and Edward plus at least one illegitimate

Notorious for his six wives, Henry was educated, charming and handsome in his youth. He invaded France and defeated Scotland at the Battle of Flodden Field in 1513. The King's fickle loyalties brought the rise and fall of brilliant advisors such as Cardinal Wolsey, Thomas Cromwell and Sir Thomas Moore. Over a lengthy reign he oversaw the break from Rome in the Reformation and the dissolution of the monasteries, which began in 1536, and the establishing of the Church of England. However, as a skilled statesman, he remained popular with his people and created a strong country.

I-SPY points: 30

Date: _____

Henry VIII was responsible for the dissolution of the monasteries; Fountains Abbey was sacked in 1539.

THE SIX WIVES OF HENRY VIII

Although a strong king, Henry VIII is best remembered for marrying six times; he had a roving eye for the pretty ladies who surrounded him at court and also wanted a son to safeguard the throne.

Catherine of Aragon

Catherine, the widow of his older brother Arthur, married Henry in 1509. Their daughter Mary was born in 1516 after two infant boys died. For years a loving husband, Henry needed a male heir and when he fell in love with Anne Boleyn, devout Catherine was cast aside. His divorce from her in 1533 marked Henry's break with the Catholic church in Rome and the establishing of the Church of England.

Anne Boleyn

Pretty Anne attracted King Henry's attention in 1526; the next year he tried to end his marriage to Catherine. She married Henry in 1533, when his advisors agreed to the divorce. Needing a male heir, her first child was Princess Elizabeth and two other pregnancies failed. Unpopular at court, she was accused of treason and beheaded in 1536.

Jane Seymour

Henry already had picked out his next queen; Jane Seymour caught his eye while serving both Catherine of Aragon and Anne Boleyn at court. She married the king in 1536 soon after Anne's execution but died the following year after giving birth to Henry's longed-for son and heir, Edward.

Anne of Cleves

Henry's fourth marriage lasted just seven months. He wanted a political alliance in Europe and looked at possible brides, including Anne of Cleves from Germany. She and Henry married in January 1540 but did not get on and they divorced in July the same year. Anne spent the remainder of her life living quietly at Hever Castle in Kent.

Kathryn Howard

The fifth wife of Henry VIII was young and foolish – and the cousin of Anne Boleyn. She was 19 when they married in late July 1540, when Henry was 49 and already fat and unfit. Soon rumours of her adultery circled the court and she went the same way as her cousin, executed in February 1542.

Katherine Parr

As Henry's health declined, he made a last marriage in 1543 to clever Katherine Parr. It was her second wedding and she believed in religious reform, clashing with courtiers who hatched a plot against her. However Henry supported her and they stayed together until he died in 1547. Katherine went on to marry Jane Seymour's brother Thomas and helped in the education of princesses Mary and Elizabeth.

EDWARD VI

Born 12 October 1537

Reign 28 January 1547–6 July 1553

Parents King Henry VIII and Jane Seymour

Children None

Under Edward's brief reign, rival nobles acted as his protector; in the power struggles, all Henry VIII's great work was undone. England went to war with Scotland and there was an economic crisis; common lands were enclosed and rents increased, leading to the Norfolk Rising in 1549. The church was in chaos and the Army was unpaid. When Edward died of consumption after seven years as king, the country was divided once more.

Edward VI, the son of Jane Seymour and Henry VIII, was born at Hampton Court.

I-SPY points: 30

<u>Date:</u>

Lady Jane Grey lived at Sudeley Castle in Gloucestershire.

 QUEEN FOR NINE DAYS

The all-powerful Protestant Duke of Northumberland named his daughter-in-law Lady Jane Grey as the new queen after the death of Edward VI. She lasted nine days before being overcome by the rightful heir, Henry VIII's daughter Mary. Northumberland was imprisoned and executed; Jane and her husband met the same fate in 1554.

MARY I

Born 18 February 1516

Reign 19 July 1553–17 November 1558

Parents King Henry VIII and Catherine of Aragon

Children None

The daughter of Catherine of Aragon was a staunch Catholic and was determined to return England to Rome. She married the Catholic Phillip II of Spain and surrounded herself with Catholic advisors, outlawing the Church of England and plunging the country into bloodshed. Protestants were executed in huge numbers, but still they rallied to the cause. Mary failed in her attempt to restore Catholicism and died childless and alone in 1558, naming her half-sister Elizabeth as successor.

How old was Mary when she gained the throne?

I-SPY points: 20, double with answer

Date: _____

Mary executed Archbishop Cranmer, who wrote the Book of Common Prayer, at Broad Street, Oxford

ELIZABETH I

Born 7 September 1533

Reign 17 November 1558–24 March 1603

Parents King Henry VIII and Anne Boleyn

Children None

The last Tudor monarch inherited a country split by religious troubles; the French and Scots had allied and all English lands in France were lost. She was an exceptional woman, clever and crafty, and popular with her subjects. Her armies helped the Protestant cause throughout Europe and Scotland and she reinstated much of her father Henry VIII's legislation. This caused friction with Spain, whose famous Armada was defeated in the English Channel in 1588. During Elizabeth's reign, great explorers sailed around the world, trade increased, William Shakespeare's plays were written and theatres built.

Whose daughter was Queen Elizabeth I?

I-SPY points: 35, double with answer

Date: _____

The original Globe Theatre in London was built in 1599, during Elizabeth's reign.

MARY QUEEN OF SCOTS

Mary was cousin to Elizabeth I and born in 1542; she spent her life in a web of intrigue. In 1556, Mary's husband Lord Darnley murdered her secretary at the Palace of Holyroodhouse in Edinburgh, and she then asked the Earl of Bothwell to kill Darnley. When this was discovered, she abdicated her throne and threw herself on the mercy of Elizabeth, who promptly imprisoned her in various noble English houses. Mary was then implicated in Catholic plots against Elizabeth, who finally beheaded her in 1587.

Mary Queen of Scots lived at the Palace of Holyroodhouse in Edinburgh.

JAMES I OF ENGLAND AND VI OF SCOTLAND

Born 19 June 1566

Reign 24 July 1603–27 March 1625

Parents Henry Stuart and Mary, Queen of Scots

Children Seven

As Elizabeth I died childless, the throne passed to James, the son of Mary Queen of Scots and the first sovereign to rule both countries. His reign was troubled, marred by religious infighting and his belief in the absolute power of the monarchy, which led to clashes with Parliament. Guy Fawkes' failed Gunpowder Plot in 1605 brought trouble between the Catholics and Puritans. However, much of the stability of Elizabeth's reign remained.

I-SPY points: 20

Date: _____

James VI was crowned at Stirling Castle in Scotland in 1567.

 Each year we celebrate a failure – Guy Fawkes' attempt to blow up the Houses of Parliament. Remember that on Bonfire Night, every 5th November.

CHARLES I

Born 19 November 1600

Reign 27 March 1625–30 January 1649

Parents James I of England (VI of Scotland) and Anne of Denmark

Children Nine

Charles I repeatedly dissolved Parliament and ruled for 11 years on his own. To raise money he levied taxes and sold titles, but by 1642 civil war had broken out, as the king battled Parliament and Puritans fought Catholics. War lasted four years, with the middle classes and merchants supporting Parliament and the nobles and peasants backing the king. Oliver Cromwell's New Model Army defeated the king at Naseby in 1645 and Charles was later executed.

I-SPY points: 25

Date: _____

The equestrian statue of King Charles I looks down Whitehall in London to the spot where he was beheaded in 1649.

OLIVER CROMWELL

Born 1599

Reign 1649–1658

Oliver Cromwell was a Puritan parliamentarian who became a Roundhead general in the Civil War of 1642–1651. He won battles in Ireland and subdued the Scots, becoming Lord Protector of England in 1653. Despite his military might, Cromwell failed to win over the English or unite the divided nation. His son Richard briefly ruled after his death but was exiled upon the Restoration of the monarchy in 1660.

I-SPY points: 35, double with answer

<u>Date:</u> _____

What were the Roundheads' enemies called?

Cromwell won a decisive victory over King Charles I at the Battle of Naseby in 1645.

CHARLES II

Born 29 May 1630

Reign 30 January 1660–3 September 1685

Parents Charles I and Henrietta Maria

Children Three plus 16 illegitimate

In 1651 Charles II marched into England with 10,000 men and suffered defeat by Oliver Cromwell; he fled to Europe until the Protectorate fell. He was invited to become king in 1660 and returned to great celebration in London. He was a weak leader and inept politician; he had many mistresses including actress Nell Gwynne. His reign saw the Great Plague and Great Fire and a two-party system introduced in Parliament.

I-SPY points: 20

Date: _____

Much of London was destroyed in the Great Fire of 1666, commemorated by the Monument in the City of London.

JAMES II AND VII OF SCOTLAND

Born 14 October 1633

Reign 6 February 1685–11 December 1689

Parents Charles I and Henrietta Maria

Children Up to ten plus seven illegitimate

Charles' brother James was a Catholic; after his accession there was an uprising by the Protestant Duke of Monmouth, which was soon crushed at Sedgemoor. Many rebels were executed and James continued to clash with his Parliament. He was so hated that his son-in-law William of Orange was invited by Parliament to become king. Landing at Brixham, Devon, he soon had the support of the country and James fled to France.

I-SPY points: 20

Date: _____

James II was briefly held in St James's Palace before he fled the country.

WILLIAM III AND MARY II

William born 4 November 1650

Reign 13 February 1689–8 March 1702

Mary born 30 April 1662

Reign 13 February 1689–28 December 1694

Protestant William was crowned with his wife Mary, daughter of James II, and the power struggles between monarch and government ended. They were haunted by Scottish Jacobite plots to restore James to the throne and won a resounding defeat over him at the Battle of the Boyne in Ireland. The Wars of the Spanish Succession saw the Duke of Marlborough emerge as a great military leader. Mary died of smallpox and William in a hunting accident.

I-SPY points: 20

Date: _____

The Old Royal Naval College at Greenwich was begun by Sir Christopher Wren in William III's reign.

ANNE

Born February 6 1665

Reign 68 March 1702–1 May 1714

Parents King James II and Anne Hyde

Children Seventeen, only one survived infancy

Mary's younger sister was married to Prince George of Denmark and had 17 children, who all died. The country thrived, thanks to the brilliance of the queen's advisors. Under the Duke of Marlborough, victories at Blenheim, Ramillies and Oudenarde won great power for England and the 1707 Act of Union with Scotland formed Great Britain. Peace in Europe came with the Treaty of Utrecht, signed in 1713.

Why did the throne pass to the German Hanover family after Queen Anne's death?

I-SPY points: 20, double with answer

Date: _____

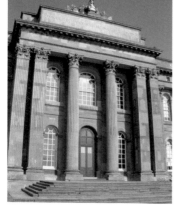

The Duke of Marlborough built his great house at Blenheim following success in wars in Europe.

GEORGE I

Born 28 May 1660

Reign 1 August 1714–11 June 1727

Parents Ernst August and Sophia Stuart

Children Two plus three illegitimate

With the death of Anne, the throne passed to the German great-grandson of James II. George I ruled over England and Hanover. He spoke no English and left the running of the country to his Whig ministers, led by the first Prime Minister, Sir Robert Walpole. In 1715 the Jacobites tried and failed to reinstate the Stuarts with the son of James II in 1720. During his reign, a financial disaster struck with the South Sea Bubble.

I-SPY points: 20

Date:

THE SOUTH SEA BUBBLE

The South Sea Company was a speculative trade venture in South America, backed by around £10 million of government money. Investors made huge profits as the share price rose and Britain went mad for shares, investing in hundreds of dodgy companies. Eventually the South Sea Company collapsed, bringing financial ruin to the country. Sir Robert Walpole was appointed the first Chancellor of the Exchequer to sort the disaster out.

The Scottish Jacobites attempted to capture Edinburgh Castle in the Rising of 1715.

GEORGE II

Born 10 November 1683

Reign 11 June 1727–25 October 1760

Parents King George I and Sophia Dorothea

Children Seven

George II left the government of Britain to the Whigs, led by Sir Robert Walpole. War was declared on Spain in 1739 and George won the Battle of Dettingen for Austrian succession in 1743. Two years later the Jacobites staged a final attempt to reinstate a Stuart sovereign, with James II's grandson, nicknamed Bonnie Prince Charlie. He was defeated at Culloden Moor in 1746. In 1756, the Seven Years' War with France led to fighting throughout Europe.

Where did Bonnie Prince Charlie escape to after the Battle of Culloden Moor?

I-SPY points: 40

Date: _____

In 1745, the Young Pretender Bonnie Prince Charlie landed in Scotland at Glenfinnan on Loch Shiel.

GEORGE III

Born 4 June 1738

Reign 25 October 1760–29 January 1820

Parents Frederick, Prince of Wales and Augusta of Saxe-Gotha

Children Fifteen, thirteen survived including George and William

For two decades, George III wrested power from Parliament, but with the loss of the British colonies in North America in the 1770s, he handed responsibility back to the government. William Pitt the Younger was appointed Prime Minister and he guided England through the French Revolutionary and Napoleonic wars, partly abolished the slave trade and united Britain and Ireland. After 1811, George was mostly insane and his son ruled as regent.

I-SPY points: 15

Date: _____

Although considered insane in later years, George III bought Buckingham House in central London in 1761 to use as home for the Royal Family, which endures today.

GEORGE IV

Born 12 August 1762

Reign 29 January 1820–26 June 1830

Parents George III and Charlotte of Mecklenburg-Strelitz

Children One plus an uncertain illegitimate

Something of a dandy, George IV was immoral and extravagant in a time when the effects of the Napoleonic War and mass industrialisation were causing countrywide social misery. He had many mistresses and loathed his wife, Caroline of Brunswick. But George was also intelligent, a great wit and a patron of the arts, commissioning John Nash to create Regent's Street and Regent's Park and turn Buckingham House into a palace.

There are lots of pubs named after the Hanover kings and queen. How many can you spot?

I-SPY points: 15

Date: _____

George IV asked John Nash to redesign the Royal Pavilion at Brighton in 1784.

I-SPY points: 15

Date: _____

King William IV was responsible for reforms in the Houses of Parliament.

WILLIAM IV

Born 21 August 1765

Reign 26 June 1830–20 June 1837

Parents George III and Charlotte of Mecklenburg-Strelitz

Children Two plus at least 10 illegitimate

Succeeding George IV in late middle age, William was a model of propriety in contrast to his decadent brother. He helped pass the Reform Act of 1832, allocating seats in parliament to industrial cities and giving the vote to some members of the newly prosperous middle classes. Slavery was abolished in British colonies in 1833 and social reforms were welcomed in a country struggling with the impact of the Industrial Revolution.

VICTORIA

Born 24 May 1819

Reign 20 June 1837–22 January 1901

Parents Edward, 1st Duke of Kent and Victoria of Saxe-Coburg

Children Nine, including King Edward VII

The niece of William IV married her German cousin, Albert, a devoted family man. After his death in 1861, Victoria withdrew from public life but not from politics; she oversaw great political and social reforms pushed through Parliament by the 10 prime ministers of her reign, including Gladstone and Disraeli. The Mines Act of 1842 forbade women and children working underground, a ten-hour working day was established and further Reform Acts widened the voting public.

An elegant memorial to Queen Victoria stands outside Buckingham Palace in London and gazing down The Mall.

Which castle in Scotland did Victoria love to holiday in?

I-SPY points: 15, double with answer

Date: _____

During Victoria's 64-year reign, the British Empire doubled in size. Wars were fought in Egypt, the Crimea and South Africa, and mutiny put down in India, but Britain was not involved in any major European entanglements. This was largely because the Queen was related to all the major royal families of Europe. Her marriage to Albert of Saxe-Coburg-Gotha was happy; his legacy is seen today in the Royal Albert Hall, Science Museum and Victoria and Albert Museum in London.

The Albert Memorial is in Kensington Gardens, London.

I-SPY points: 15

Date: _____

EDWARD VII

Born 9 November 1841

Reign 22 January 1901–6 May 1910

Parents Queen Victoria and Price Albert

Children Five including George V

Ascending the throne aged 59, Edward VII proved to be a skilled diplomat, in contrast to his wasted years as dissolute heir to the throne. Foreign affairs were his forté and in an uneasy Europe heading for war, the Entente Cordiale with France in 1904 was largely Edward's initiative. He passed a raft of social reforms, introducing free secondary education, old-age pensions and labour exchanges, and laying the basis for National Insurance.

Who was Edward VII married to?

I-SPY points: 20, double with answer

<u>Date:</u> _____

There is a memorial statue of King Edward VII in Centenary Square, Birmingham.

GEORGE V

Born 3 June 1865

Reign 6 May 1910–20 January 1936

Parents Edward VIII and Alexandra of Denmark

Children Six including Edward VIII and George V

The second son of Edward VII faced political crisis throughout his reign; two elections in 1910 saw the power of the House of Lords reduced. The First World War broke out in 1914, followed by partition in Ireland, with Dublin establishing an independent government in 1922. Social unrest led to the General Strike in 1926 and the world economic crisis in 1929–1931 caused mass unemployment throughout the 1930s. George also oversaw the introduction of self-rule in British colonies.

I-SPY points: 35

Date: _____

George V died at Sandringham House in Norfolk on 20th January 1936.

WORLD WAR I

World War I started in July 1914 when an Austrian aristocrat, Archduke Franz Ferdinand was assassinated by Serbian terrorists and ended in November 1918. In that time, over nine million people were killed. At first the old enemies in Europe were involved: Germany, Austria, Italy, France and Britain, but fighting spread across the globe to China, Japan, the Middle East, the Pacific Rim and North Africa. Russia caved in after the October Revolution in 1917 and the following year the Americans joined the Allies (France and Britain) to force the Germans into retreat. Peace was declared on 11 November 1918.

EDWARD VIII

Born 23 June 1894

Reign 20 January 1936 – abdicated 11 December 1936

Parents George V and Mary of Teck

Children None

Months into his reign, Edward VIII sparked a crisis by proposing marriage to American divorcée Wallis Simpson, going against his position as head of the Church of England, which was opposed to remarriage by divorcées. Britain talked of nothing else, despite the looming threat of war and two million unemployed. On 10th December 1936, Edward VIII abdicated. He and Mrs Simpson married, became the Duke and Duchess of Windsor and moved overseas.

I-SPY points: 25

Date: _____

The Cenotaph was built by Sir Edwin Lutyens to honour the dead of World War I.

The Duke and Duchess of Windsor are buried side by side behind Frogmore Mausoleum in Windsor Park.

How does Great Britain remember the war dead every November?

WORLD WAR II

World War II started in 1939 when Germany invaded Poland. France and England then declared war on Germany; at its peak 61 countries were involved in the fighting. Hitler was the German leader, Churchill the great English Prime Minister who took Britain to victory in 1945. In those six years, London and many British cities were bombed and over 60 million people were killed worldwide; many were Jews in German concentration camps.

In 1940, Coventry Cathedral was destroyed in a German bombing raid. This new cathedral opened in 1962.

GEORGE VI

Born 14 December 1895

Reign 11 December 1936–6 February 1952

Parents George V and Mary of Teck

Children Two including Queen Elizabeth II

Edward VIII's younger brother worked hard to improve the reputation of the monarchy after the Abdication Crisis of 1936, but this was overshadowed by the outbreak of World War II. At its end, King George VI and Queen Elizabeth were loved by the nation for visiting troops, the front line, factories and bomb-damage victims. After the war, the National Health Service was created, as well as the Bank of England. Some transport and energy companies were brought under public ownership in a nationalisation programme.

Who became queen on the death of George V in 1952?

I-SPY points: 25

Date: _____

King George VI and Queen Elizabeth the Queen Mother are interned in the north nave aisle of King George Chapel.

Index

First published by Michelin Maps and Guides 2012 © Michelin, Proprietaires-Editeurs 2012. Michelin and the Michelin Man are registered Trademarks of Michelin.

Created and produced by Blue Sky Publishing Ltd. All rights reserved. No part of this publication may be reproduced, copied or transmitted in any form without the prior consent of the publisher. Print services by FingerPrint International Book production – fingerprint@pandora.be.

The publisher gratefully acknowledges the contribution of Sasha Heseltine who wrote the text and of the I-Spy team: Camilla Lovell, Geoff Watts and Ruth Neilson in the production of this title. The publisher also gratefully acknowledges the contribution of Chris Tweed, Martin Silverston, Finlay McWalter, The Royal Collection, Players, Cigarette Cards - National Portrait Gallery, BBC/Corbis, www.visitcardiff.com, The Camera Press, Sasha Heseltine, Sudeley Castle, Glastonbury Abbey and Unitaw Limited who provided the photographs in this book. Other images in the public domain and used under a creative commons licence. All logos, images, designs and image rights are © the copyright holders and are used with kind thanks and permission.

10 9 8 7 6 5 4 3 2 1

Answers: P9: Tettenhall: Wolverhampton. **P10:** Malmesbury: Gloucestershire. **P13:** Vikings: from Scandinavia: Denmark, Norway and Sweden. **P15:** Harold: because he was nimble and fast in battle. **P17:** Harold, by an arrow in his eye. **P18:** a way to divide up the land. **P21:** Blois: France. **P24:** Magna Carta: Big Charter: red. **P33:** Warwick: the find to influence who ruled the country. **P35:** Tudor rose: white. **P37:** Henry VIII: Catherine of Aragon. **P41:** Mary: 37. **P42:** Elizabeth: daughter of Henry VIII and Anne Boleyn. **P46:** Roundheads: Cavaliers. **P50:** Anne: the Hanovers were the nearest relations with claims to the British throne. **P52:** Bonnie Prince Charlie: Isle of Skye in the Inner Hebrides, Scotland. **P56:** Victoria: Balmoral Castle. **P58:** Edward VI: Princess Alexandra of Denmark. **P61:** war dead: with red poppies. **P62:** George VI: Queen Elizabeth II

63

HOW TO GET YOUR I-SPY CERTIFICATE AND BADGE

Every time you score 1000 points or more in an I-Spy book, you can apply for a certificate

HERE'S WHAT TO DO, STEP BY STEP:

Certificate

- Ask an adult to check your score
- Ask his or her permission to apply for a certificate
- Apply online to www.ispymichelin.com
- Enter your name and address and the completed title
- We will send you back via e mail your certificate for the title

Badge

- Each I-Spy title has a cut out (page corner) token at the back of the book
- Collect five tokens from different I-Spy titles
- Put Second Class Stamps on two strong envelopes
- Write your own address on one envelope and put a £1 coin inside it (for protection). Fold, but do not seal the envelope, and place it inside the second envelope
- Write the following address on the second envelope, seal it carefully and post to:

I-Spy Books
Michelin Maps and Guides
Hannay House
39 Clarendon Road
Watford
WD17 1JA